Sports Training Not Volleyball

MW01113356

This Book Belongs to:

_____

_____

_____

_____

Reward If Found:

_____

_____

© 2010 JoeDolanPR / LayFlat Sketchbooks
9663 Santa Monica Blvd
#612
Beverly Hills, CA 90210
www.SportsTrainingNotebooks.com

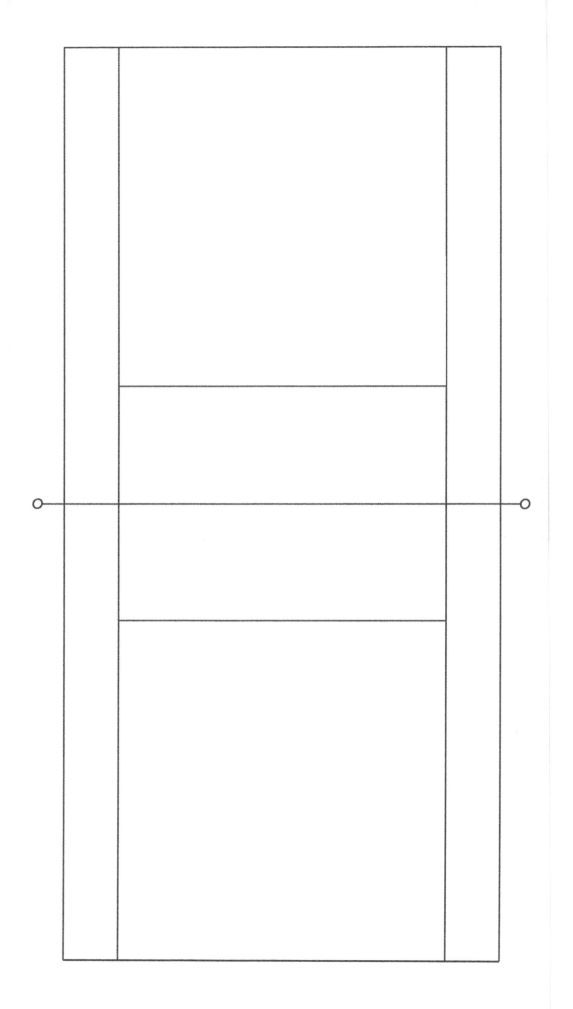

Date:

Notes:

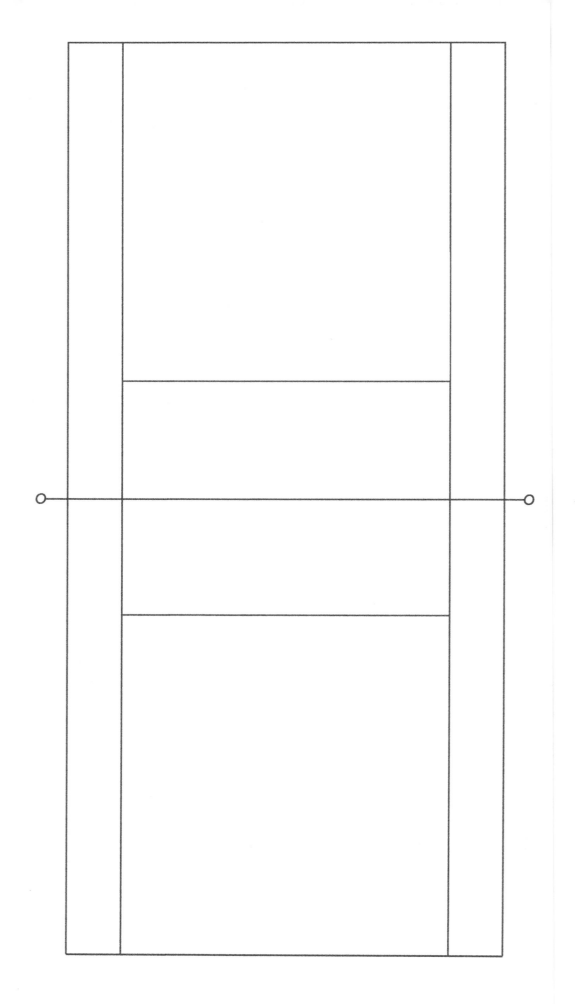

Date:

Notes:

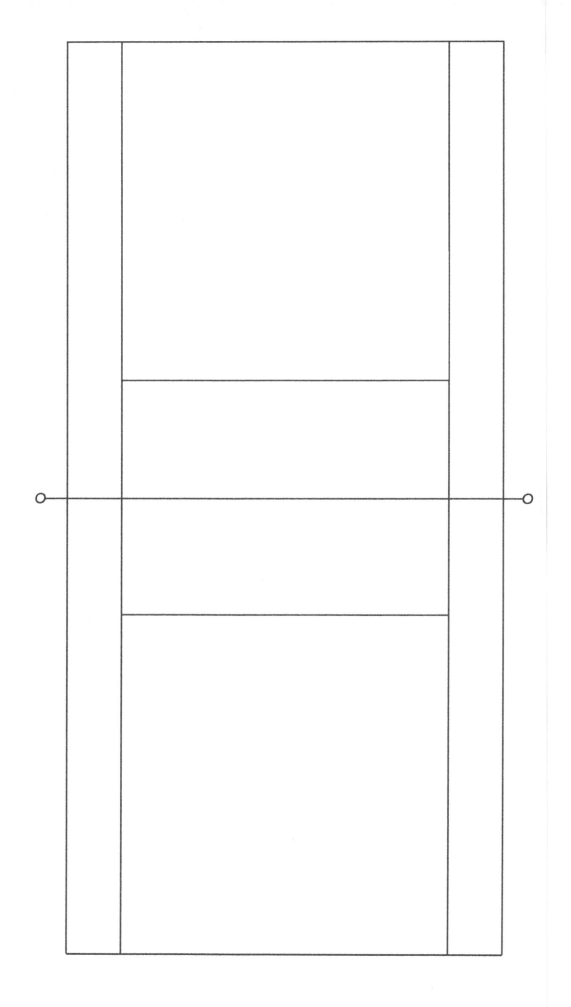

Date:

Notes:

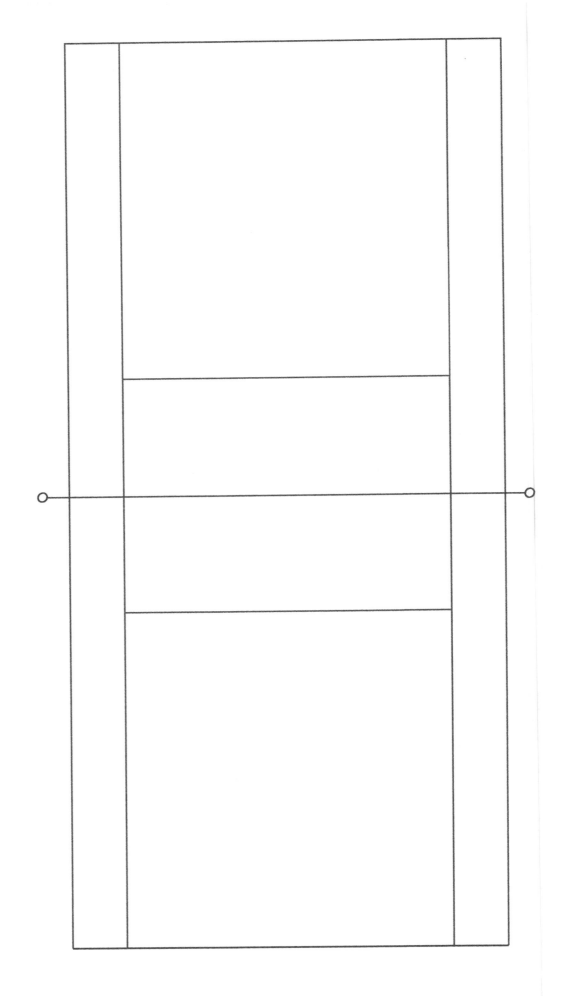

Date:

Notes:

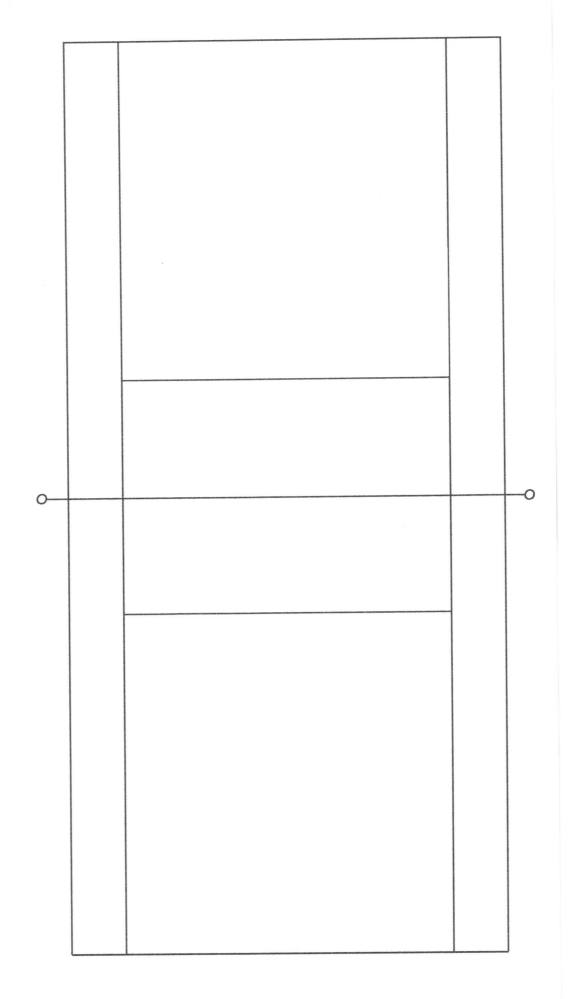

Date:

Notes:

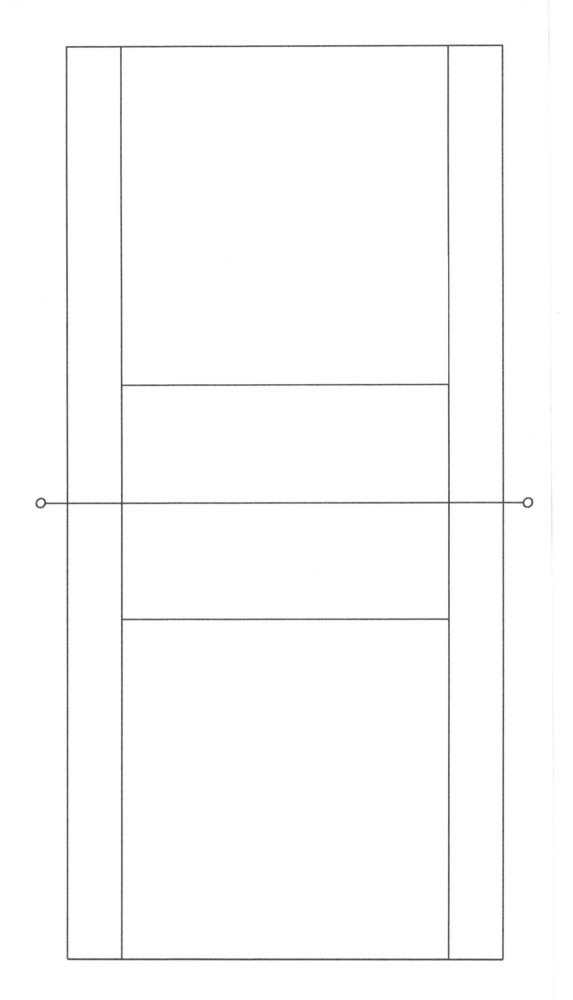

Date:

Notes:

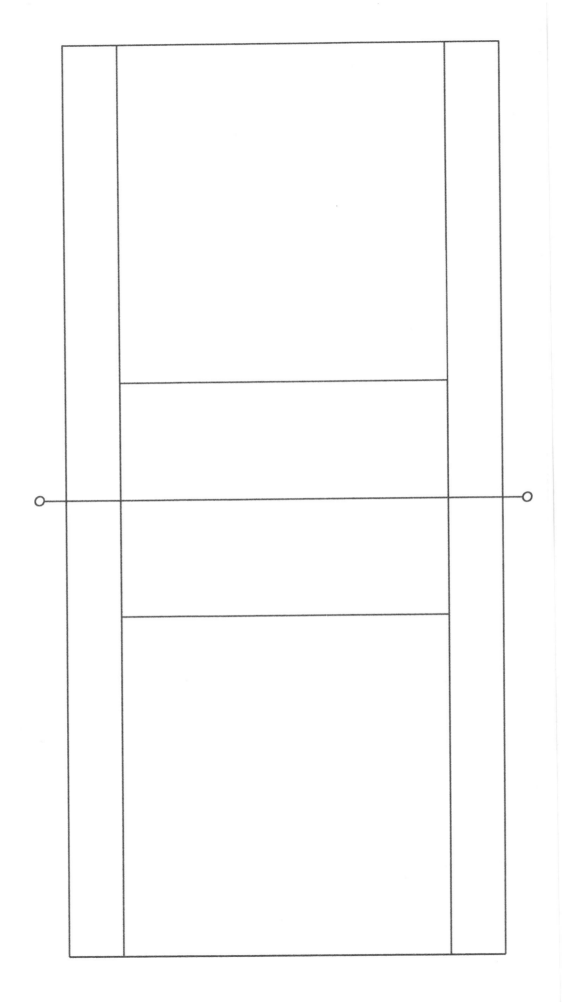

Date:

Notes:

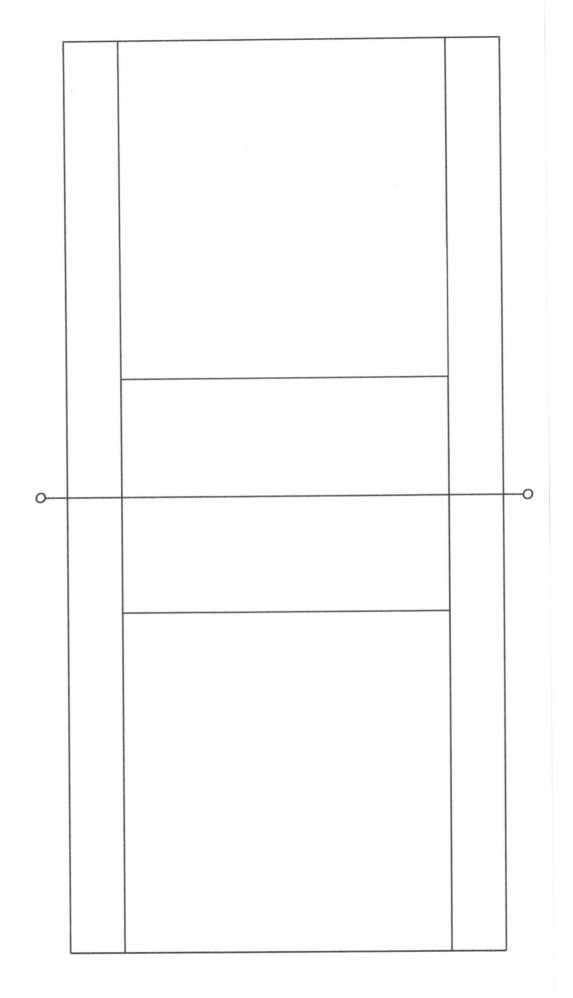

Date:

Notes:

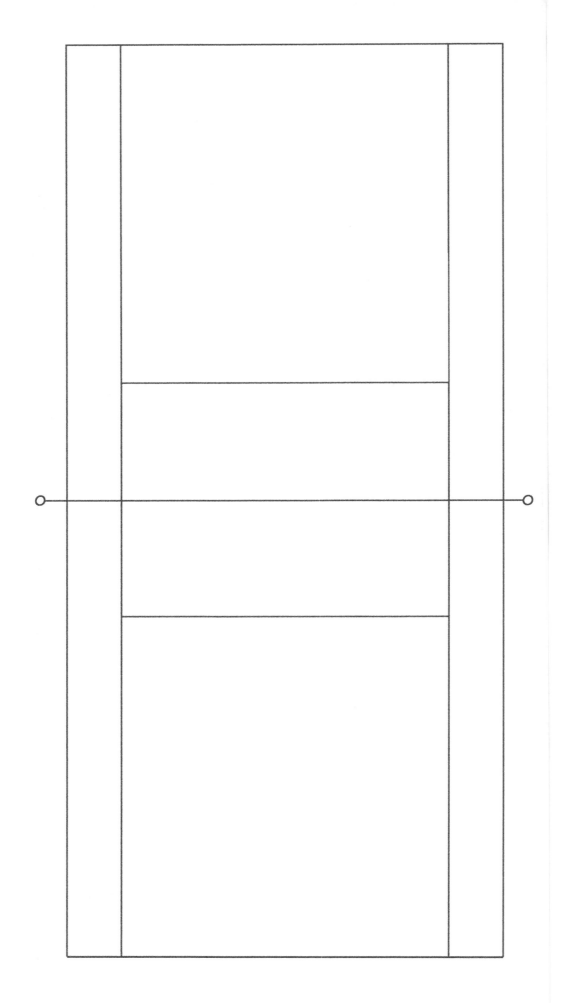

Date:

Notes:

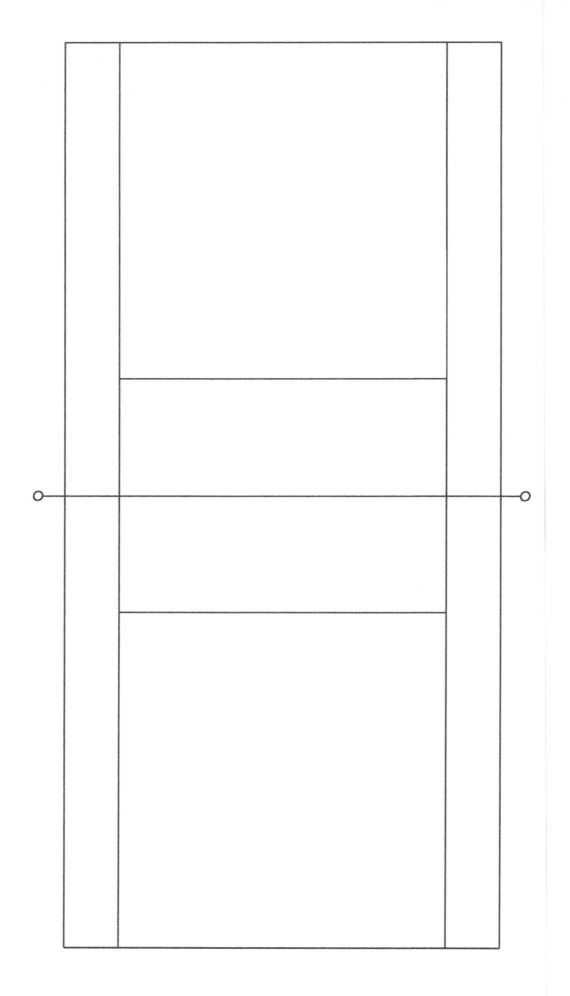

Date:

Notes:

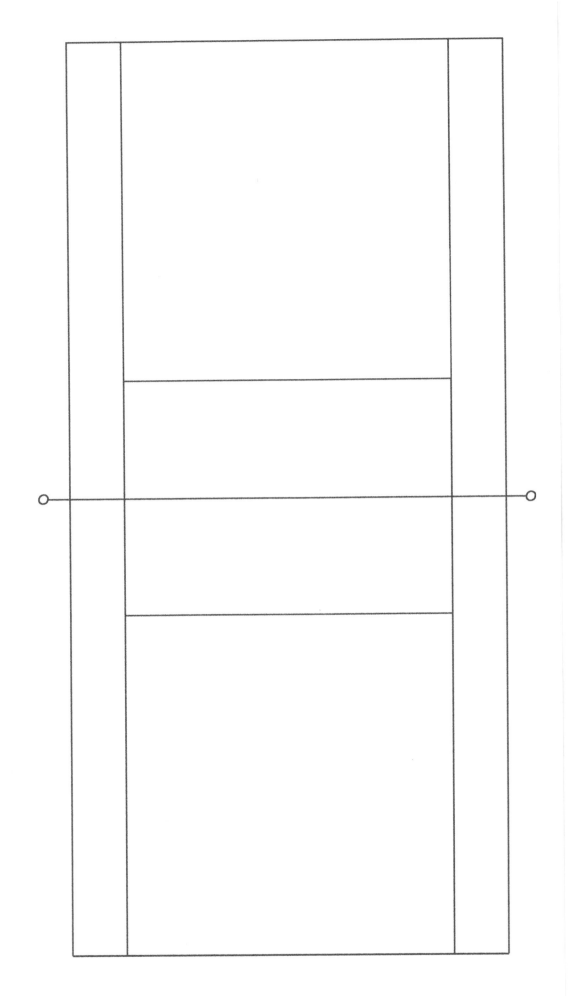

Date:

Notes:

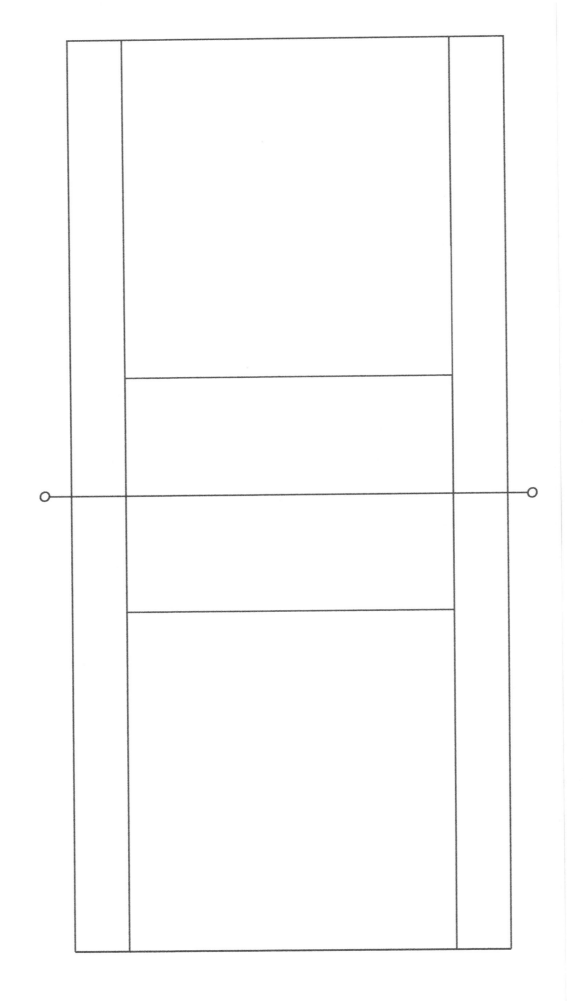

Date:

Notes:

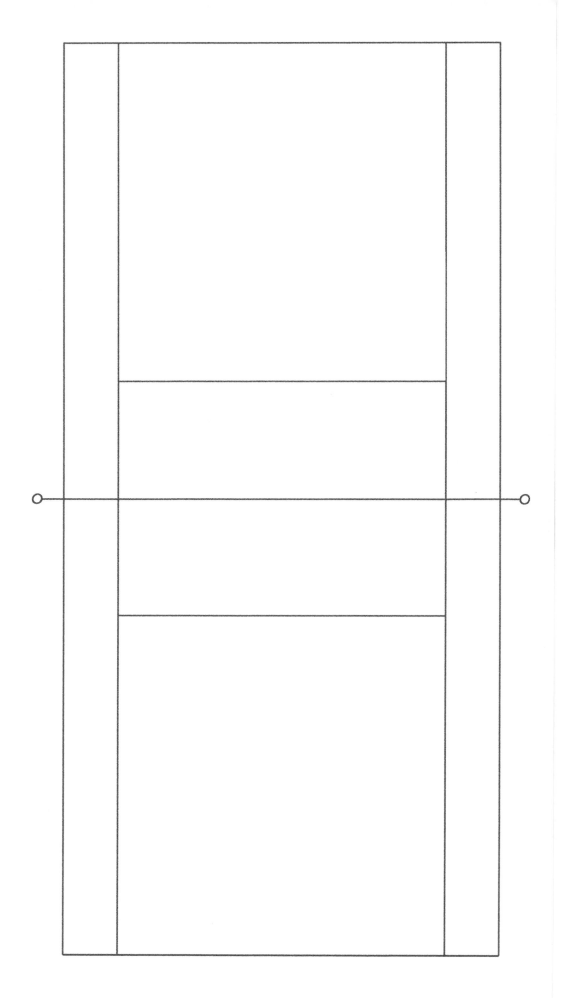

Date:

Notes:

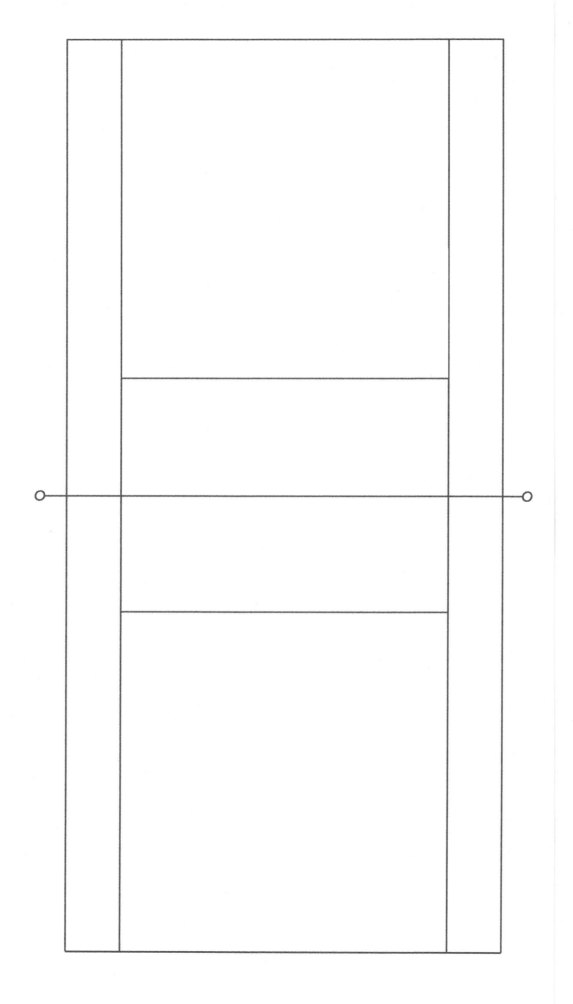

Date:

Notes:

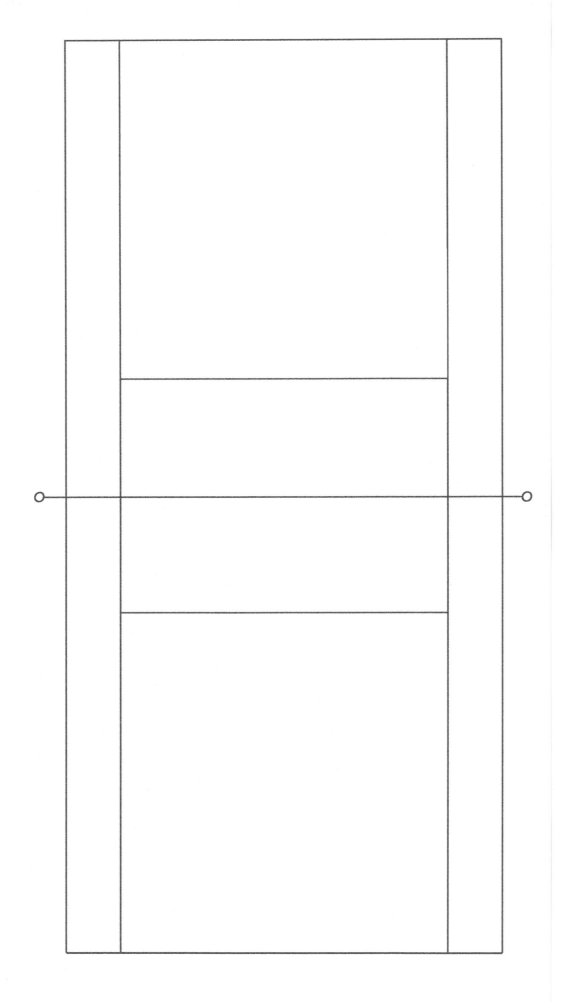

Date:

Notes:

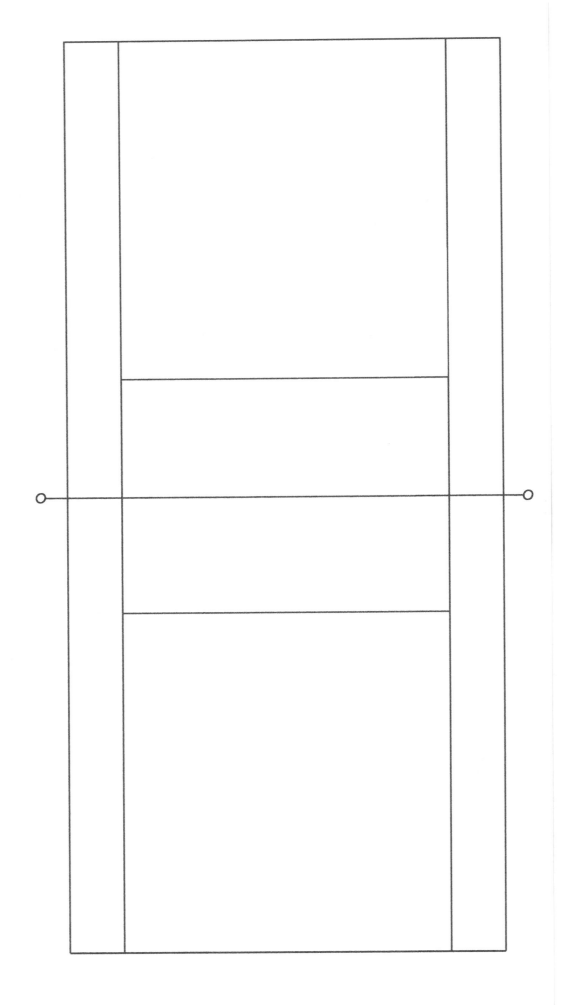

Date:

Notes:

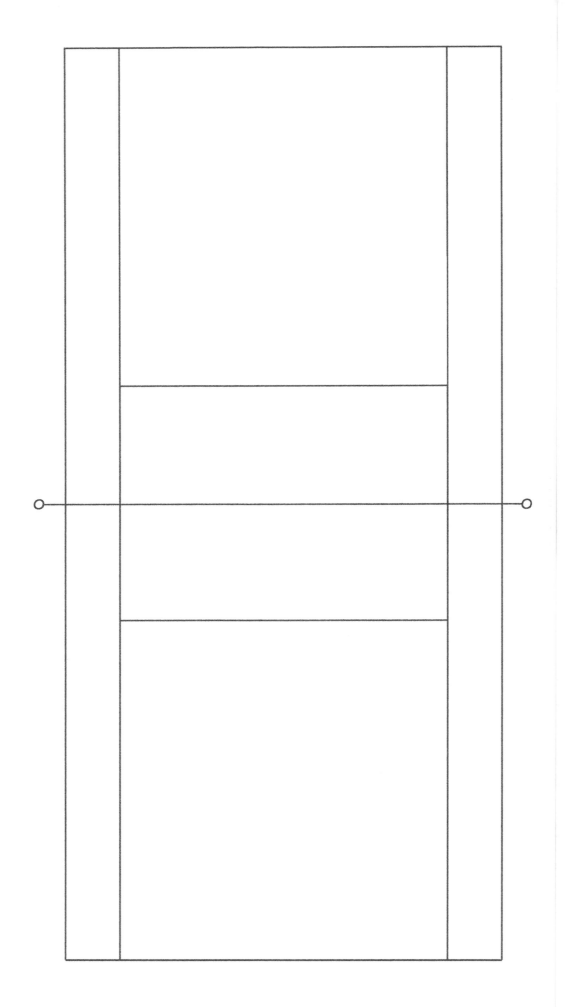

Date:

Notes:

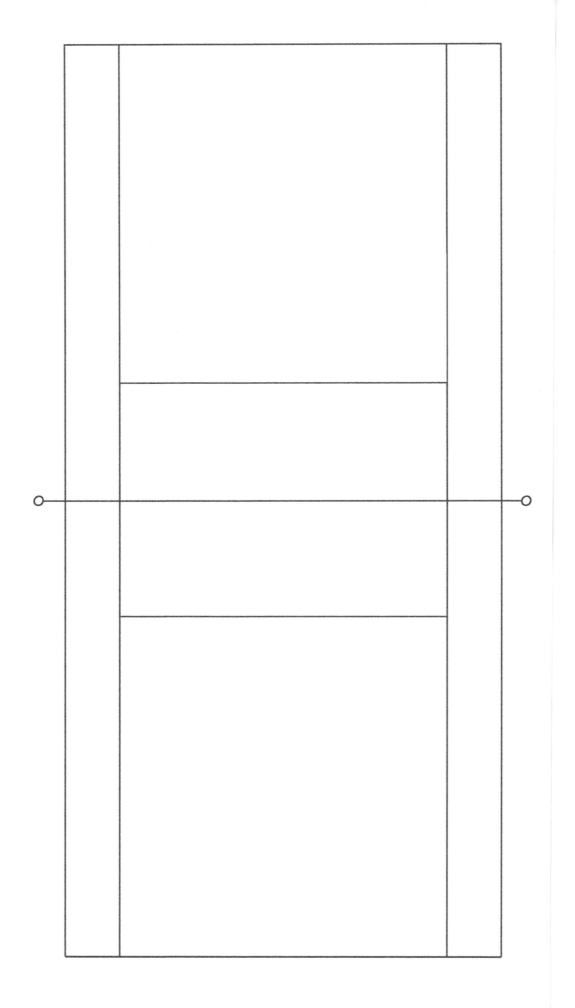

Date:

Notes:

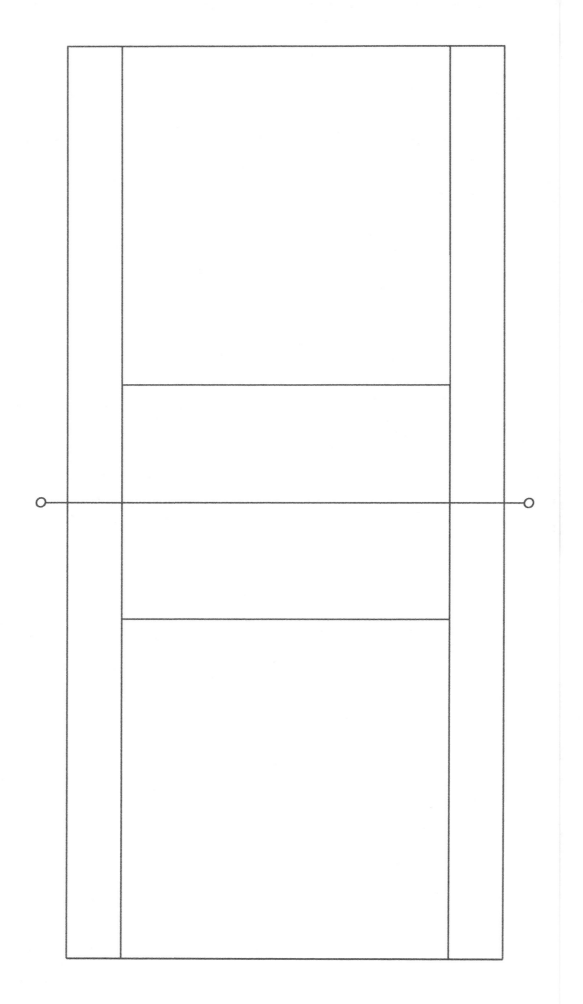

Date:

Notes:

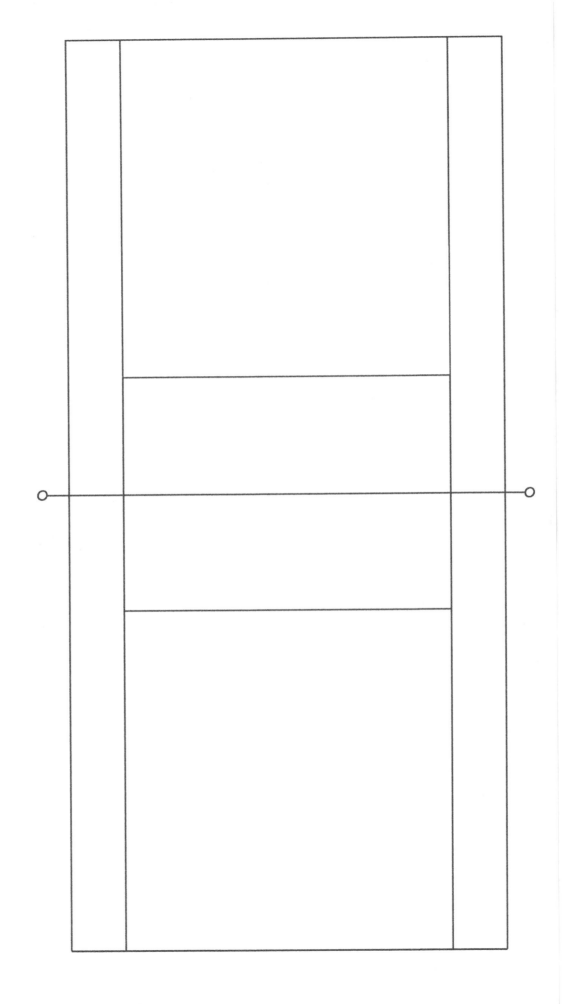

Date:

Notes:

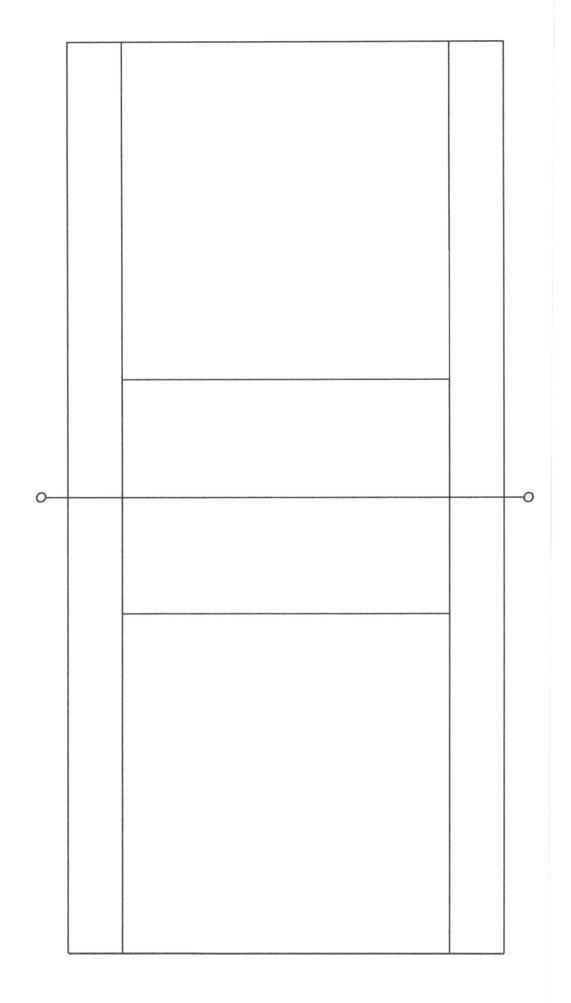

Date:

Notes:

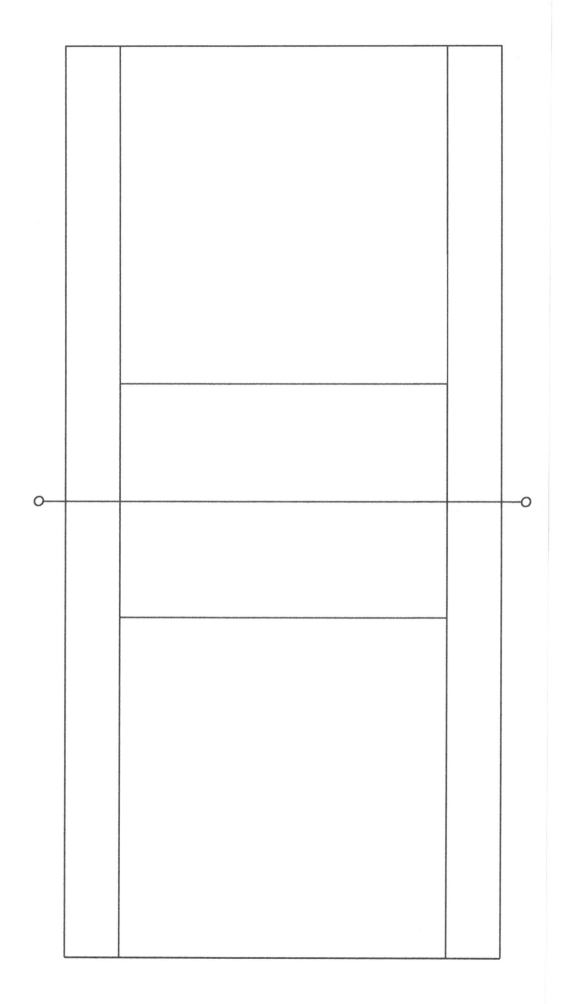

Date:

Notes:

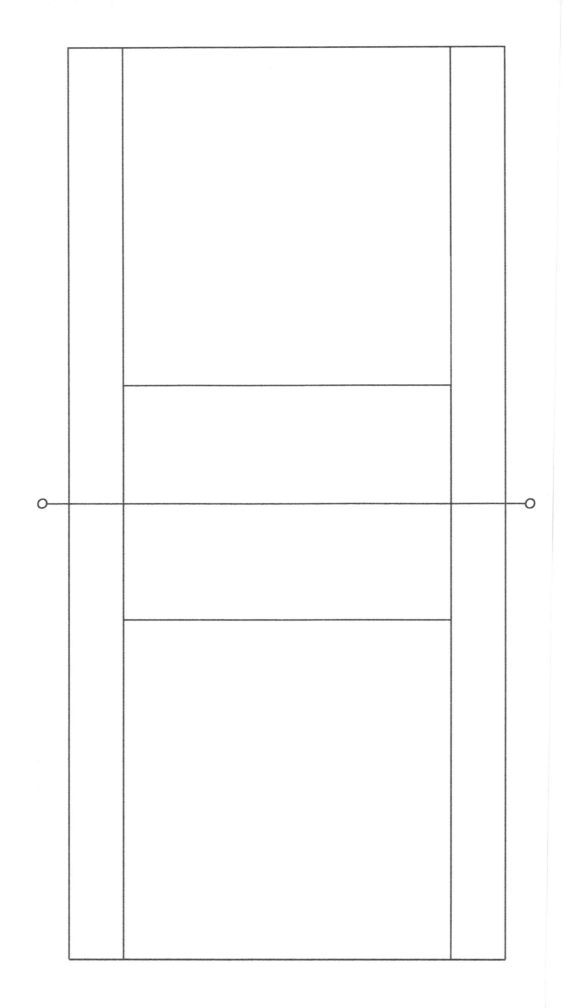

Date:

Notes:

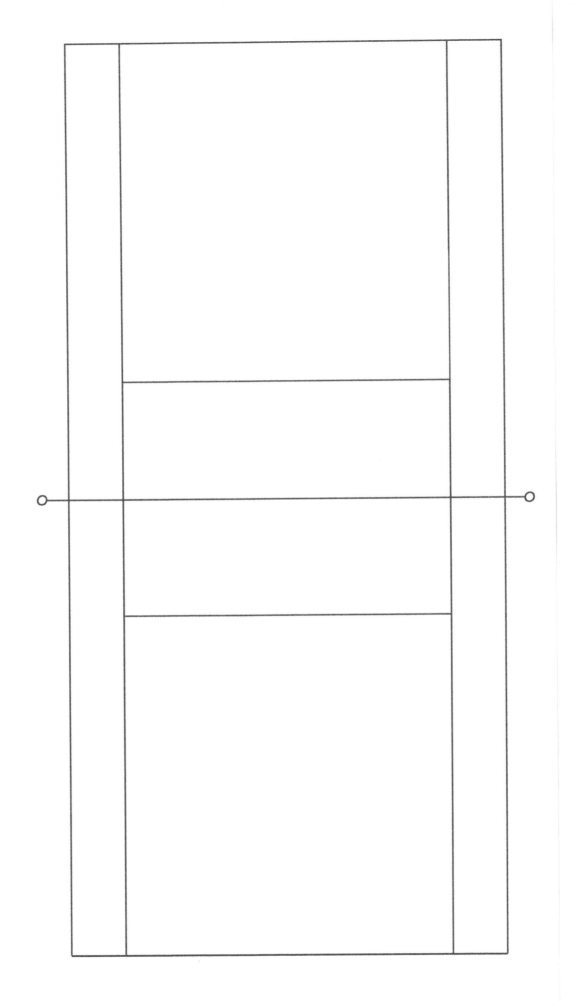

Date:

Notes:

Date:

Notes:

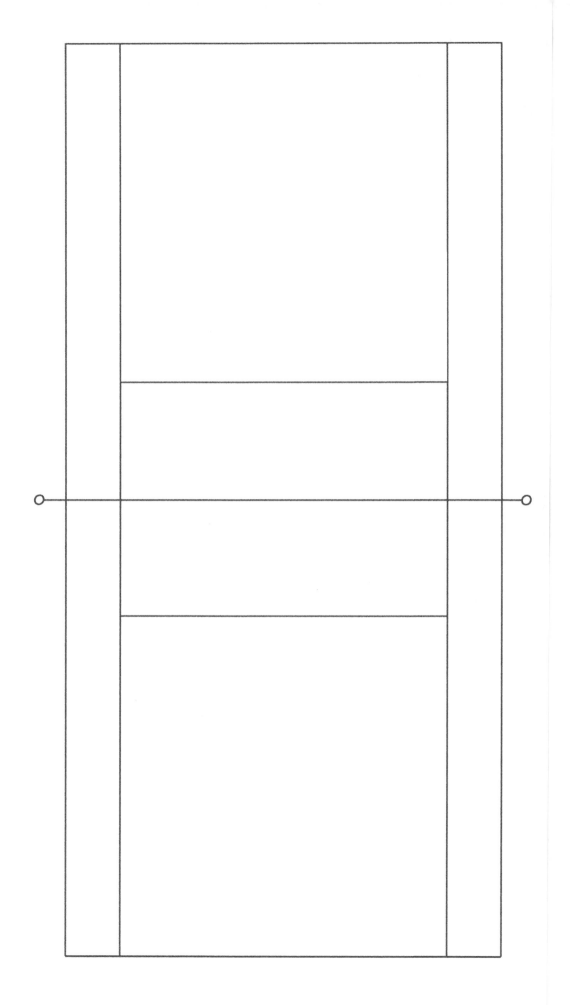

Date:

Notes:

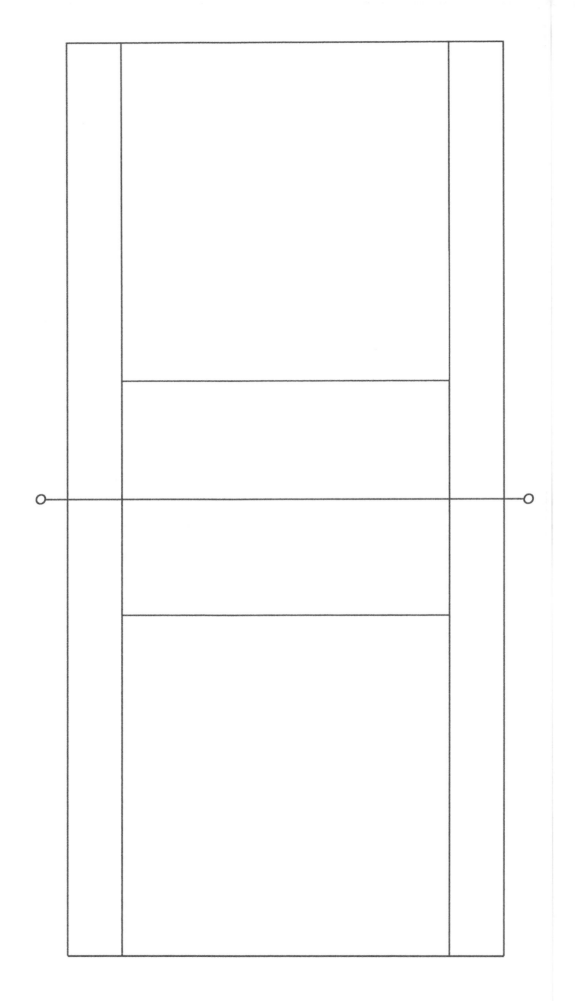

Date:

Notes:

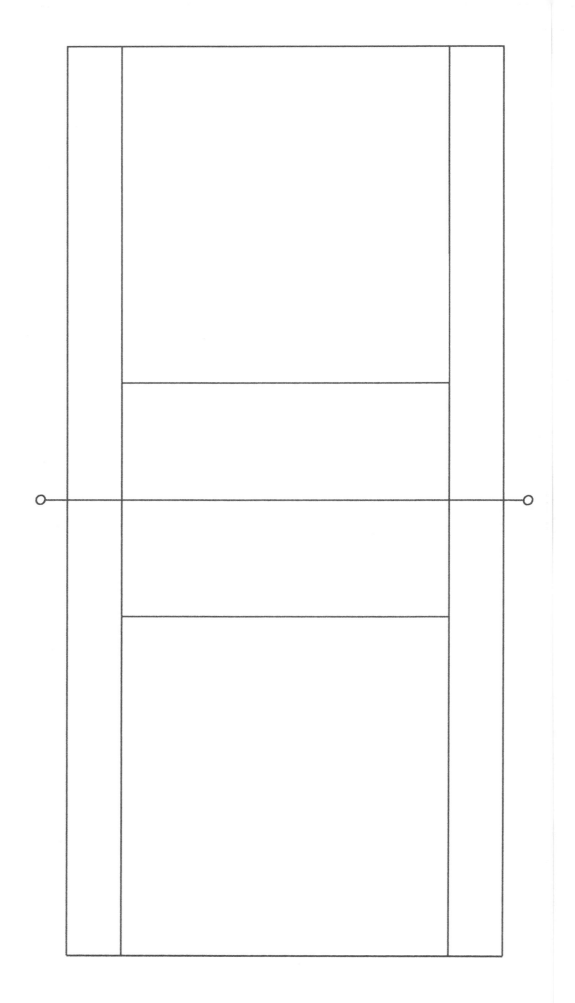

Date:

Notes:

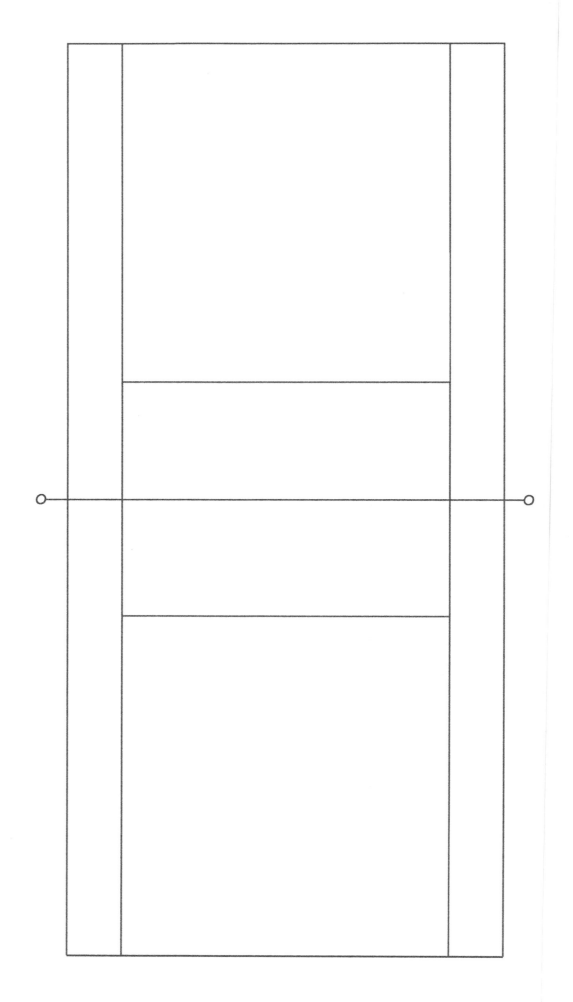

Date:

Notes:

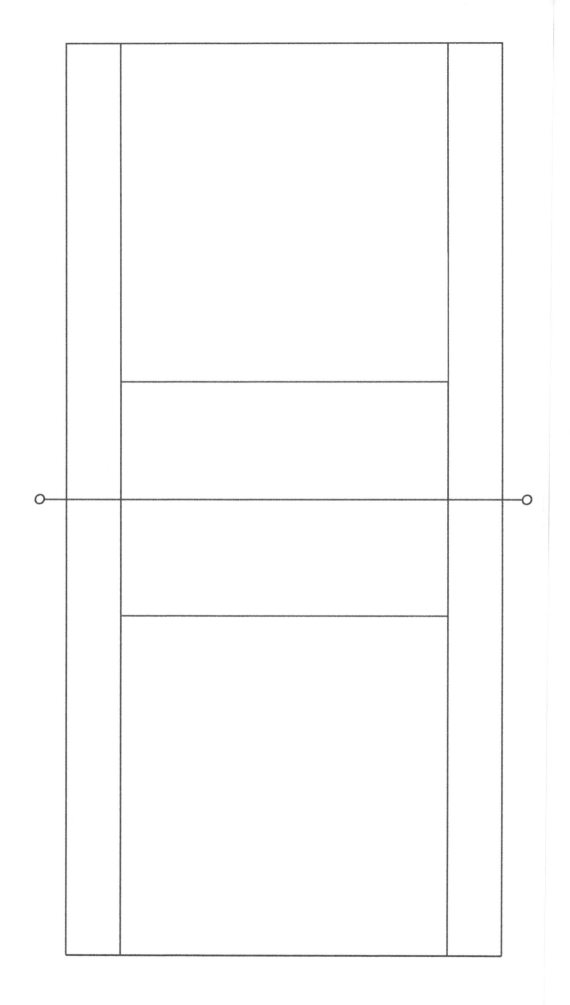

Date:

Notes:

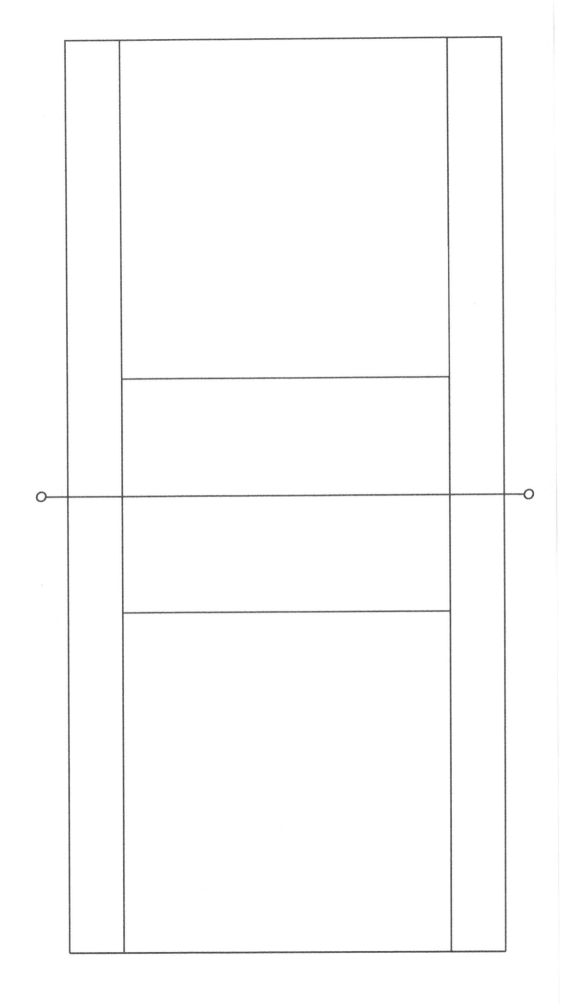

Date:

Notes:

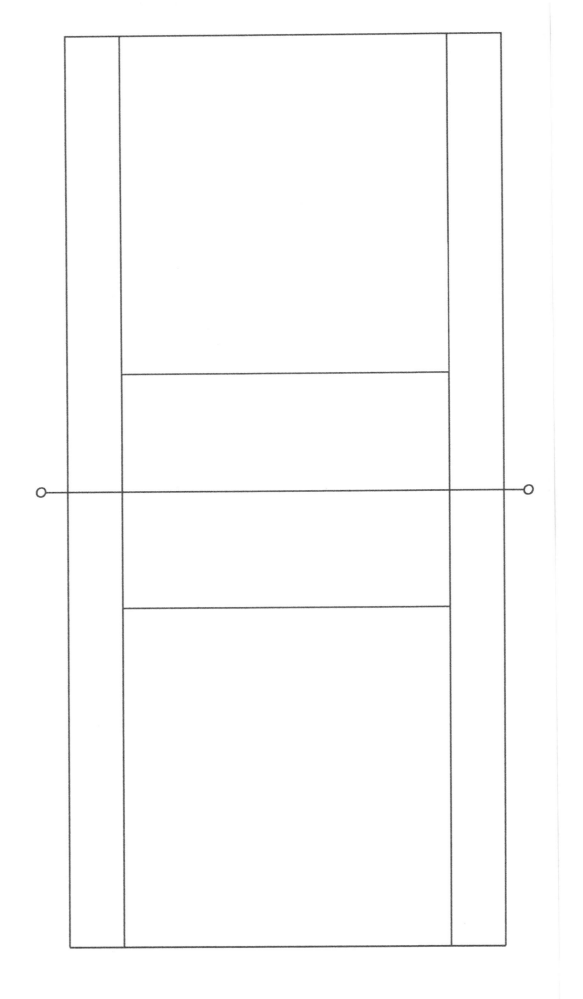

Date:

Notes:

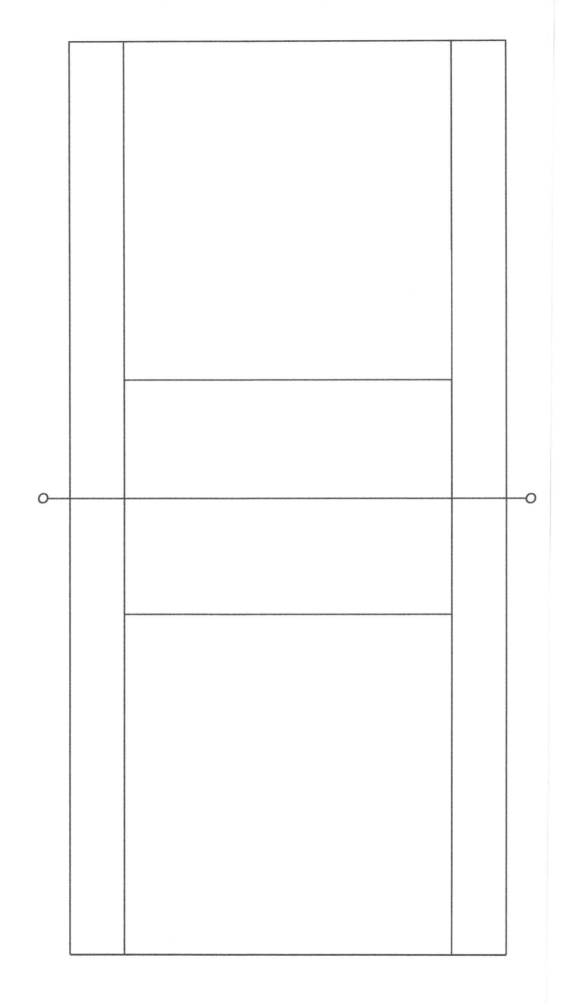

Date:

Notes:

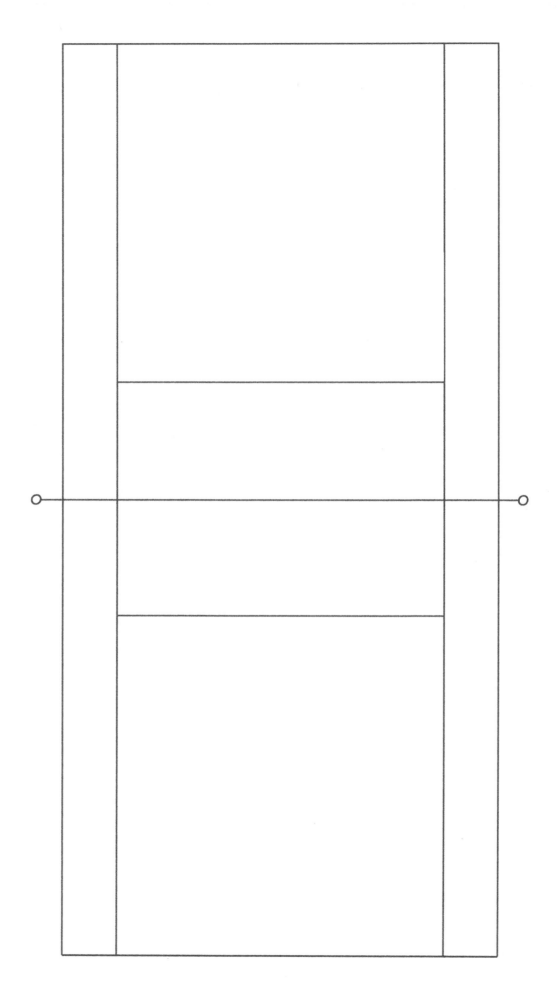

Date:

Notes:

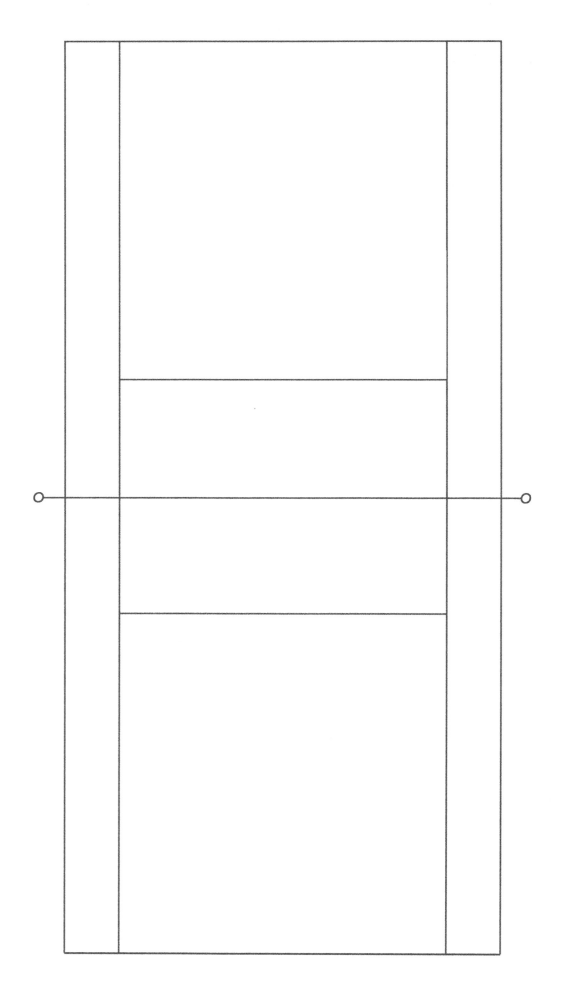

Date:

Notes:

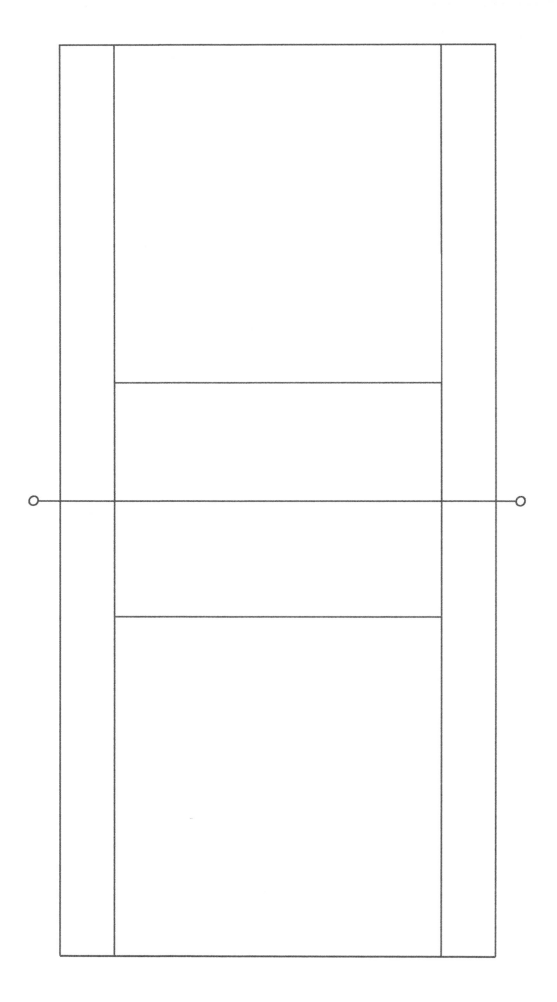

Date:

Notes:

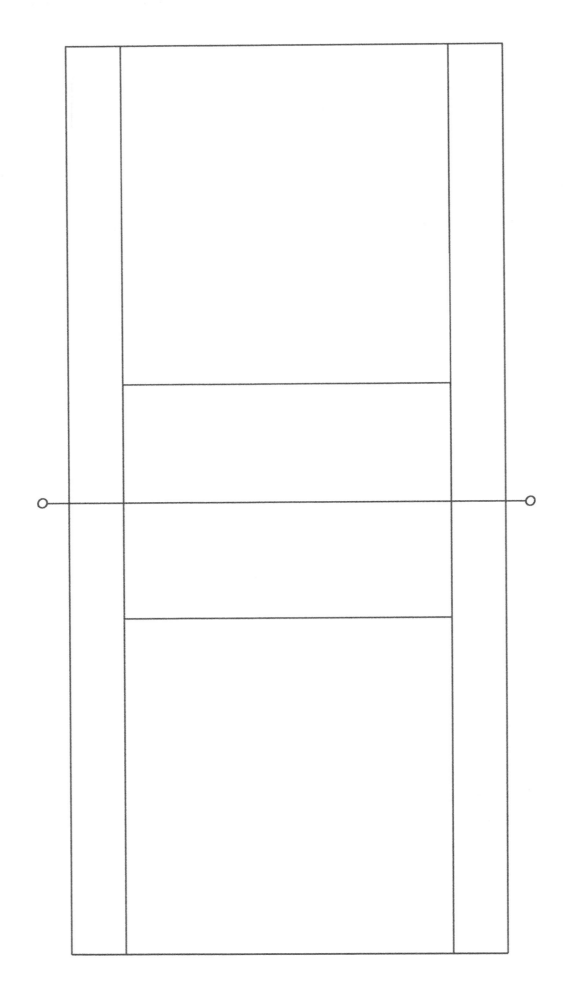

Date:

Notes:

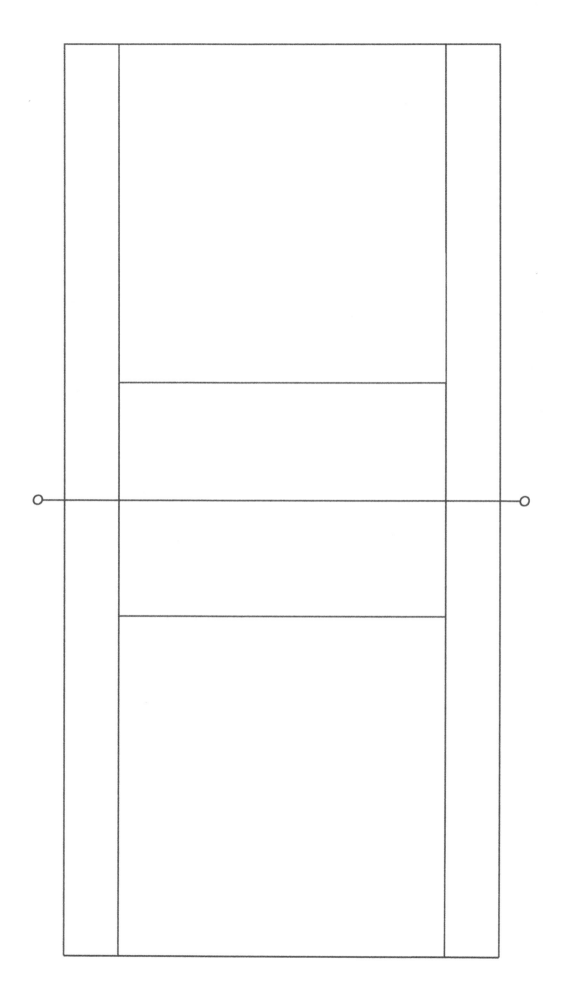

Date:

Notes:

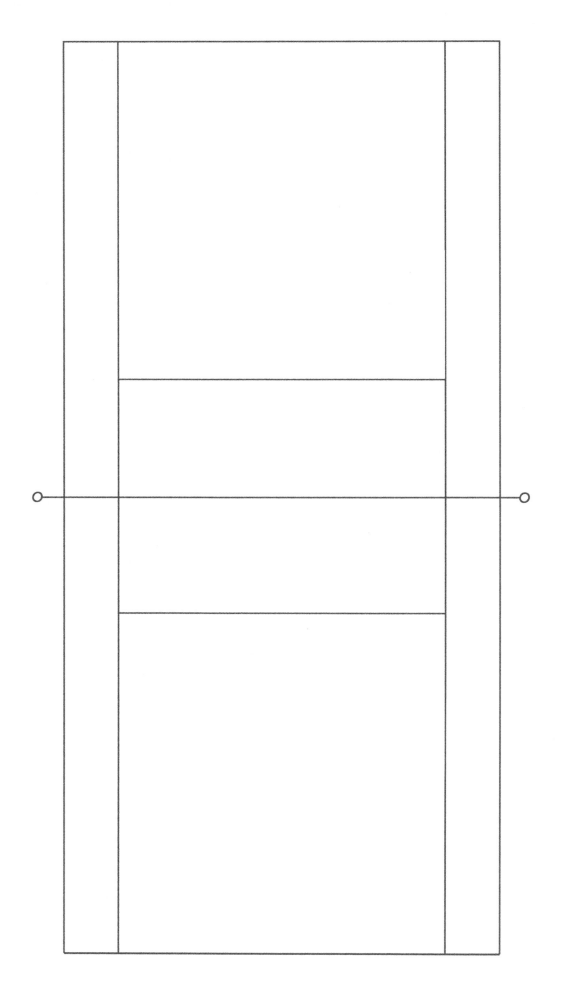

Date:

Notes:

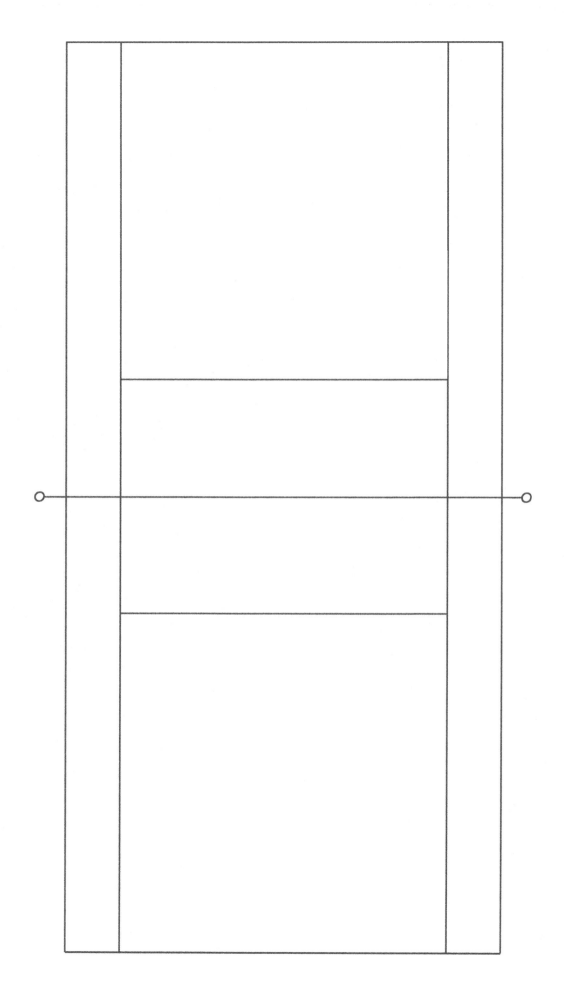

Date:

Notes:

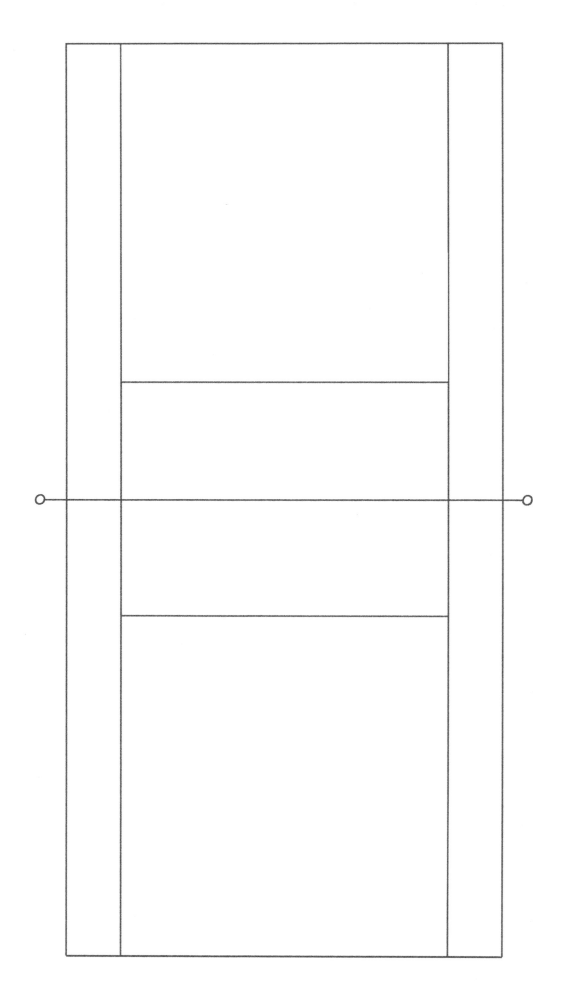

Date:

Notes:

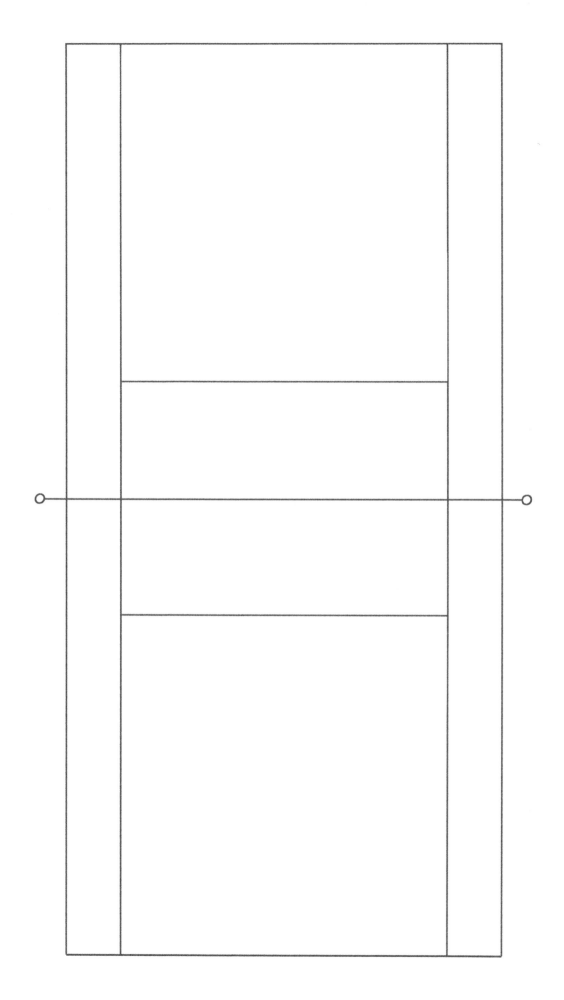

Date:

Notes:

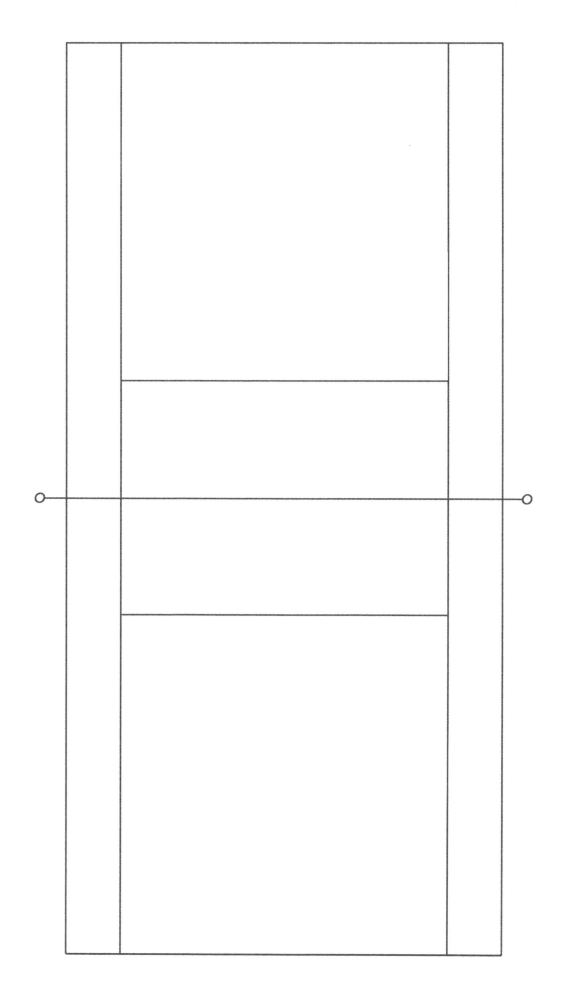

Date:

Notes:

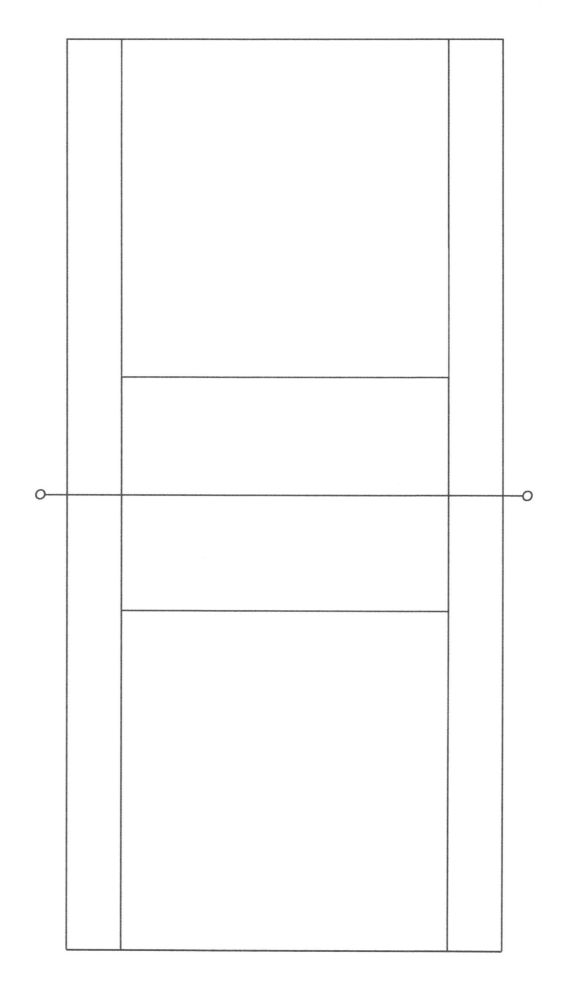

Date:

Notes:

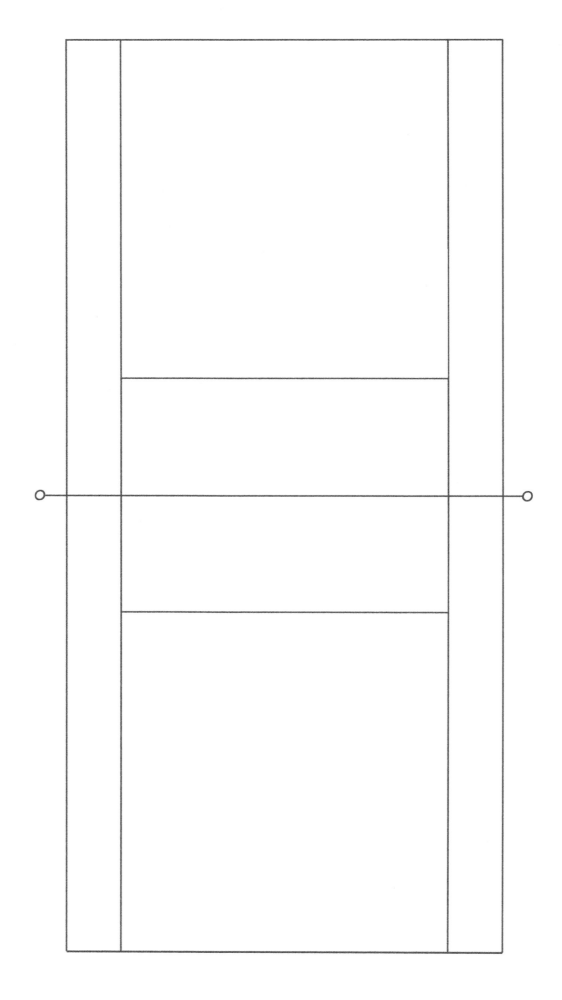

Date:

Notes:

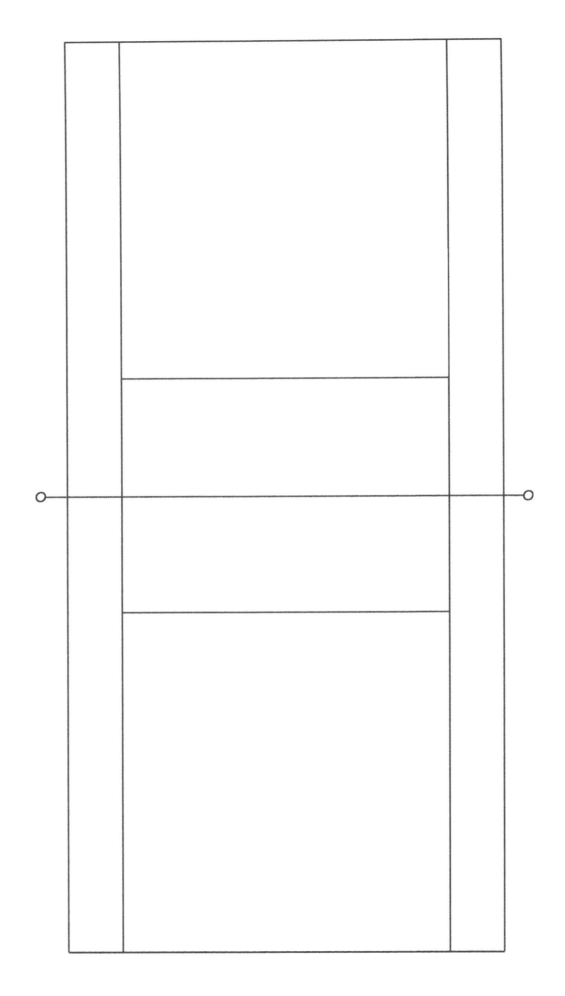

Date:

Notes:

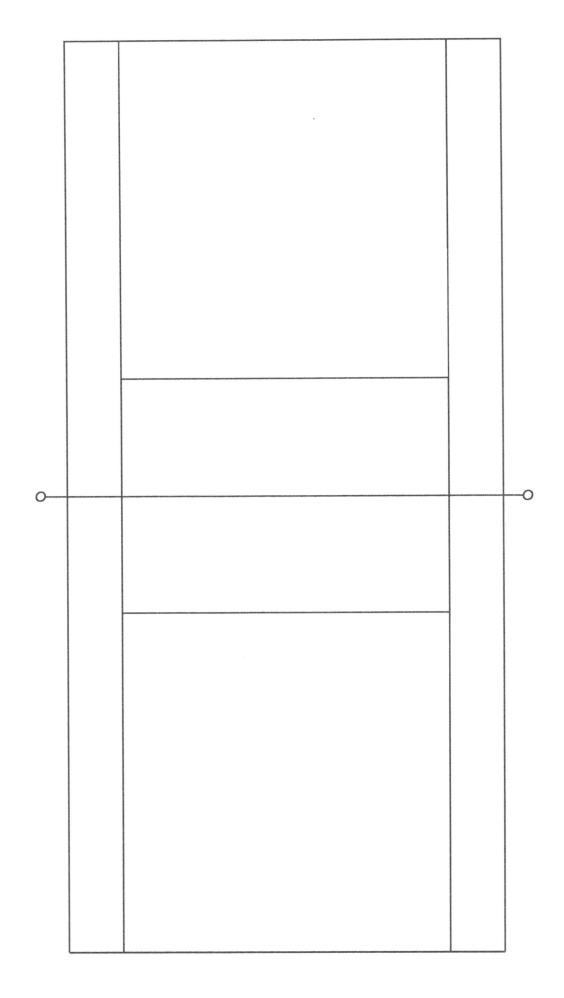

Date:

Notes:

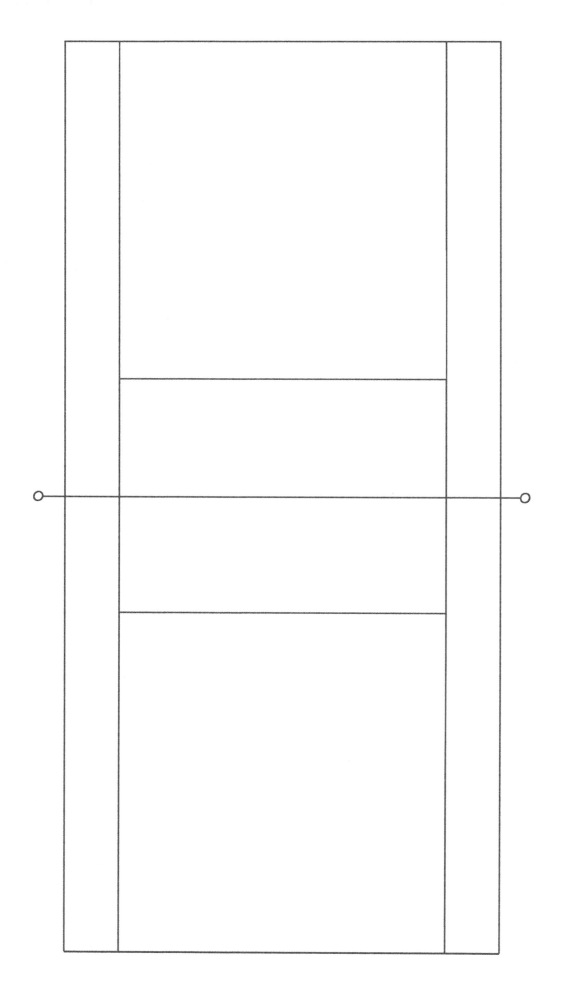

Date:

Notes:

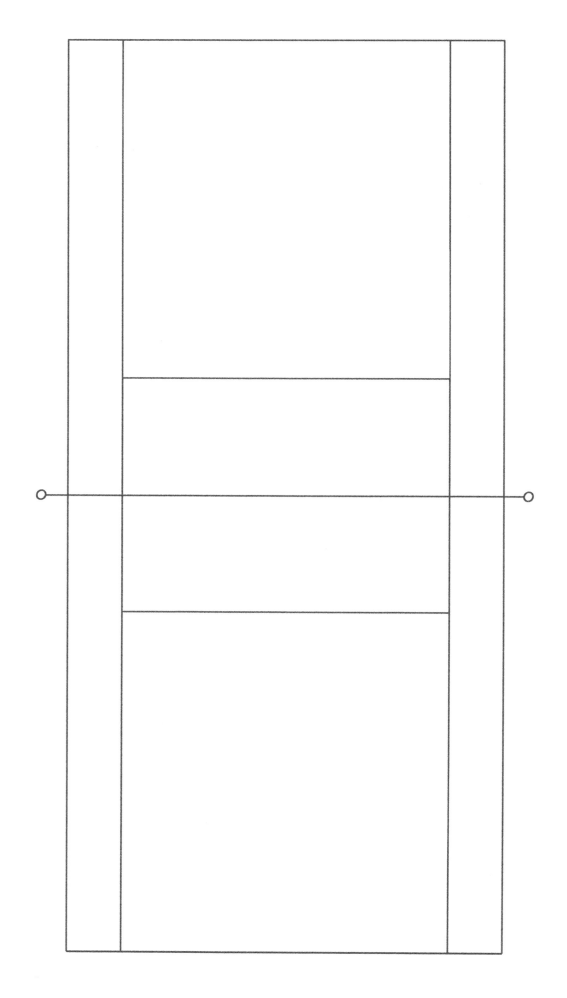

Date:

Notes:

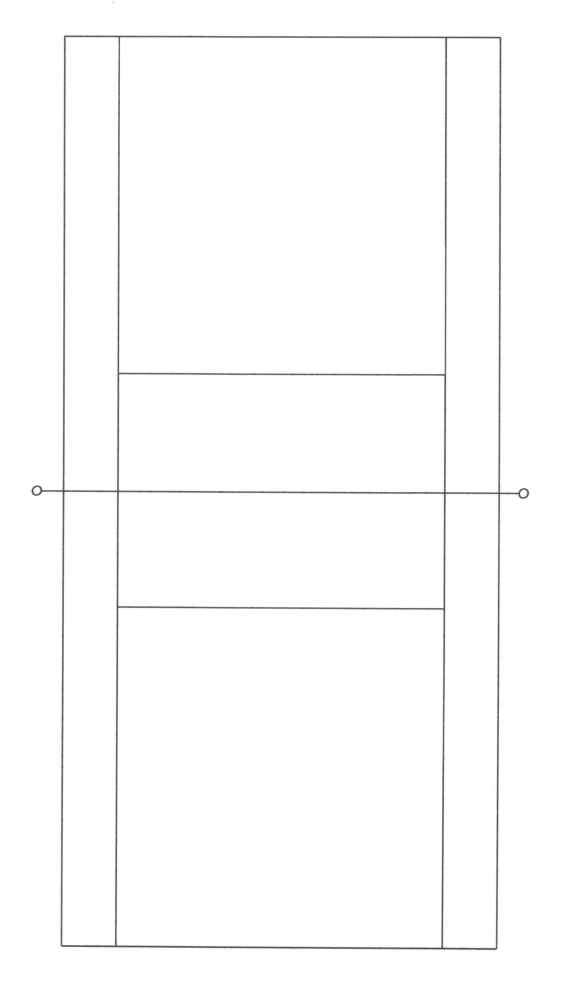

Date:

Notes:

	MONDAY	TUESDAY	WEDNESDAY	THURSDAY	FRIDAY	SATURDAY	SUNDAY
6:00							
6:30							
7:00							
7:30							
8:00							
8:30							
9:00							
9:30							
10:00							
10:30							
11:00							
11:30							
12:00							
12:30							
1:00							
1:30							
2:00							
2:30							
3:00							
3:30							
4:00							
4:30							
5:00							
5:30							
6:00							

Locker Number: _____   Lock Code: _____

Coach: _____   Coach's Telephone: _____

96930944R10057

Made in the USA
Middletown, DE
02 November 2018